Jim Harrison

HIS WORLD REMEMBERED

"Art without emotion has no meaning. Subject matter is extremely important to me. I have much love and respect for every object I paint."

Jim Harrison

Jim Harrison

HIS WORLD REMEMBERED

Written by Gary C. Dickey

Published by
American Masters Foundation
Houston, Texas
1982

First Edition

Published in the United States of America by American Masters Foundation, Inc., 1982

Printed by Hart Graphics, Inc., Austin, Texas

CONTENTS

COLOR PLATES

ACKNOWLEDGMENTS

Many people helped make this volume a reality. While a number of them have been mentioned elsewhere in this book, I wish to add a special word of thanks to all others who gave so unselfishly of themselves. I shall always value highly their friendship, wise counsel and generosity.

Especial thanks are due my publisher, Randy Best, and American Masters Foundation; my trusted business manager, Dave Cullen; my secretary, Rosie Lee, who assisted in the gathering of materials; Vicki Abstance, for typing and preparation of the manuscript; Dorothy Murrell, who has a knack for knowing just how it should be done; Beth Dickey, for her kind assistance and professional help in editing and proofreading; Gary Dickey for the superb writing; Frame House Gallery, my print publisher, for allowing me to use most of the paintings in this volume; and to my wife Margaret for her encouragement throughout my art career.

DEDICATION

To my mama 'cause she bought me my
first art kit and much much more . . .

A WORD FROM THE ARTIST

It never crossed my mind that I was beginning a fine arts career back in the summer of 1949 when I first climbed that sign painter's scaffold on the side of McCartha's Hardware in Denmark, South Carolina. The Coca-Cola sign that J. J. Cornforth and I started that day was the first of some 100 similar signs I painted with that elderly gentleman over the next few years. Mr. Cornforth had a small sign painting business. His early instruction only concerned teaching me the art of sign work, but that was my first art instruction, and it fascinated me. However, the fascinations of youth are too often subdued by the realities of adulthood. My early thoughts of being an artist were gradually pushed into the back of my mind as I was constantly reminded that I was foolishly dreaming. It was not until I was thirty-five years old that I started dreaming like a child again and made the decision to pursue art full time. Fortunately, from that point on I no longer made decisions based on logic. With a lot of good luck, and the help of some wonderful people, I'm able to do what I want to do.

I sincerely feel that every Jim Harrison painting has a little bit of many people in it. Surely there are traces of my teachers, Miss Zita Mellon, Oscar Wetherington, and Mr. J. J. Cornforth, who so patiently taught me my trade. I hope that in my paintings my mother can see some evidence of the many sacrifices she made to get me through college. Her many hours of overtime night work as a telephone operator to get extra money are as much a part of each painting as are the hours and brush strokes that I now put in them. I will long remember how cautiously she counted out the $20 for my first real art kit. Neatness and precision in my work reveal the lessons taught me by my daddy, who was truly an artist in his own line of work. He had to labor hard all his life and insisted on his three boys working. It was from him that I learned the value of hard work and the pride in doing a good job. My wife Margaret contributes in an important and unique way. She and I know that her expressed confidence at the right time is as important to me as are the brushes and paints.

I am often asked if I am trying to say something with my work. Most of my painting efforts these past years have been for the purpose of perpetuating things; times and places of the past. To label me just a barn and sign painter is not fair. I must have tremendous feeling for my subjects, but I am also concerned with the "spirit" of the place or thing.

I think I'd prefer being called a "mood painter". Without trying to be classed as one delivering a social comment, I do feel that I am making my statement for posterity...a posterity that would, in many ways, have been cheated by our so called "progress". Very little of our American heritage of yesteryear remains unspoiled by pollution and undamaged by the bulldozer. It is my purpose to stay a little ahead of the wrecking crews so that I may record as much about the yesterdays and yesteryears as possible. This book is a part of that effort.

Jim Harrison

INTRODUCTION

There are times in our lives when the full significance of events is not evident until examined in retrospect. We find, sometimes years afterward, that a seemingly inconsequential occurrence — a chance meeting, perhaps—comes to play a far greater role in our lives than we ever would have imagined. Such has been the case in my association with Jim Harrison.

Somewhat faded now, the memory of our first meeting comes back from time to time. It has been almost ten years since I received the assignment to write the first magazine article ever done about the artist from Denmark, South Carolina. I tried hard to make my mark as a freelance writer, while Jim took his first faltering steps to rise in the ranks as a painter.

I smile now when I think back on it, because the events leading up to that interview were so typical of the man I later came to know and admire. In our first contact by telephone, I sought to arrange a mutually suitable time for the interview. Although we lived 50 miles apart, Jim said, "Sharpen your pencil, I'll be there inside an hour."

Of all impressions one might get from a visit with Jim Harrison, it is a picture of determination and drive, tempered with quiet understanding. One discovers quickly that here is a man who understands the old verities, the truths that make this life worth the struggle it sometimes is.

But at the same time, there is a melancholy sadness which pervades any relationship with the artist. It is a sadness borne by the realization of the deeper task to which the artist is committed: to capture the moment and hold back, if only briefly, the flood of time. Certainly no one is fully capable of doing that, but there is a dignity in striving to do so, and Jim's art comes as close as anything can.

I have followed his career since our first meeting and in the present work I have delved perhaps deeper than was necessary for a biography of this scope, but I have done so in a search for the origin of feelings evoked by the artist's works—feelings that many may quickly dismiss as "nostalgia" or "reminiscences."

They are more than this, certainly. Regardless of the labels we place on them or what our backgrounds may be, we will all find a part of ourselves pictured in this volume. And, in the end, there may be a reluctance in turning the pages to go on—reluctance perhaps best expressed in the following lines by Ralph W. Seager:

. . . In these splendid brief moments of passing through a gate, we find ourselves at the in-between interval of leaving and arriving, caught in the instant with one step in the past and the other in the future, being neither here nor there, but in a strange new time.

Gary C. Dickey

Brown Branch Cabin
McCormick, South Carolina

THE EARLY YEARS

Some things will remain forever in our memories. Even from childhood the feelings, faint impressions, sounds and smells will return in later years and bring with them the warm recollection of close ties. The sensation that comes with the changing seasons will carry a meaning that goes deeper than the moment. The touch of moist earth in the shadow of rambling kudzu, with its distinctive summer-sweet scent, serves to return the artist to an almost forgotten time and place…a place he remembers as home.

Home for Jim Harrison in the early years was the southwest Georgia town of Leslie. It was the home of his mother and most of her kin, only a few miles from Plains, where a future President also was growing up.

Life began in the large white house on the corner with the huge porch which went all the way across the front and down the side. It had large round columns and was supported by brick pillars almost six feet above the ground.

"When I picture my granny's house in my mind, I'm standing now in the street out front, and I suppose it looked much the same on that night, January 11, 1936, when I was born. There was a street light on the corner, not on a pole like today, but strung from a cable, a large bare bulb under a flat reflector."

In the shadow cast by the reflected light lay the young artist's world — the old brick retaining wall covered with green moss and always moist—the paths that ran beside the wall, and the hedge which in spring would explode with thousands of tiny white bugs when shaken by a small boy full of wonder.

There was no grass in the yard—just dirt, a common characteristic of the rural South. Jim's grandmother would keep the yard swept bare, even the backyard where grew the fig tree, the chinaberry, the pear and the scuppernong arbor. Not far from the barn was the outhouse — there was no indoor plumbing.

"And I remember a woodpile and a big black pot where the Negro woman, Rosetta, would boil the water on wash day, stirring it with a big stick and using lots of lye and rough soap. That's a vivid picture in my memory of Rosetta stirring the wash pot while Grandma swept the yard with stick brooms bound together with torn strips of cloth."

Leslie was home, but only infrequently. Most of the family's living was done on the road—a succession of boarding houses, hotels, and one-night accommodations all over the Southeast, as Harrison and his mother followed the nomadic path of his father, a telephone lineman helping with the great southward expansion of telephone lines.

"We were everywhere during those days. I don't remember much about the travel itself. We were in and out of more boarding houses than I care to remember. It was always a makeshift sort of thing with mother cooking on a hot plate—always moving in and out. But at the same time, it was exciting for me as a boy."

Alabama, Florida, Mississippi, Georgia, Louisiana, Kentucky, and Tennessee. The states were a kaleidoscope of changing landscapes connected by the long march of telephone poles pushing ever deeper into the remote backcountry of the South. For the youngster who watched it all, with a sense of adventure in his heart, the names held a certain magic, like Dunnelon, Citronelle, and Crystal River, or Slidell, Waycross, and Tuscaloosa.

From the mountainous Great Stone Gap to the flat sand beaches of Ft. Pierce, Jacksonville, or St. Augustine, through the red clay hills of the Carolinas and Georgia, westward through Alabama to the lazy deltas of Mississippi and Louisiana. It was a time of travel, watching and learning—never staying in one place for long.

"My dad was involved in building new lines—expansion. With his gang, they would build a line all the way across the state of Florida. They might be working on a project like that when news would reach us that a hurricane had blown the lines down in Mississippi. On one day's notice, we would move to Mississippi to repair the damage."

Although the hectic pace was oftentimes hard, there were the good times as well. Most often Saturday was a time for socializing, when the gang would get together for a barbecue in the mountains or a fish fry on the banks of a Florida river. As the only youngster in a crowd of forty or fifty adults, the younger Harrison enjoyed the attention he received.

"We did all kinds of things like that. And wherever we happened to be, Daddy would take me shopping at the dime store on Saturdays. There seemed to be just millions of toys at the dime store, and I thought that a dollar was a lot of money to have to spend on Saturday.

"One of the things that stands out most in my memory of those days was my first haircut. I don't know how old I was at the time, three or four at the most, and I don't remember where we were. But I do remember Daddy carrying me into the Barber Shop with its strong smell of lotions and shaving soap and the shoeshine chair in the corner. Barbershops at that time were the same throughout the South.

"At the time I had lots of curly hair and took some measure of kidding about it. Many times I was mistaken for a girl, and some thought I was Shirley Temple.

"I can still remember that barber taking out that wooden board and putting it across the arms of the barber chair. I sat up on that board and endured the haircut, but I was scared...really scared."

If things were hard on the road, it all seemed more than worth it when the small family would finally pack up and turn the big truck toward home, to the relatives and friends who waited in Leslie. There were many occasions when Jim and his mother would visit in Leslie while the elder Harrison continued traveling. Just as he had been born there in his grandmother's big, white house on the corner, so were two younger brothers, Phil and Wendel. And these were occasions for extended stays.

If you had stood on the platform of the small railroad station on a summer day in 1941, and looked back, you could just about see the whole town of Leslie. It was small by any standard, with a population of less than 500. It was linked to the rest of the world by a single railroad track which carried the "Doodlebug" as the train was called, through Leslie on its way to Americus twelve miles away. In the gathering dusk of evening, you could set your watch by the "Doodlebug's" whistle as it returned heading east toward Savannah.

At the end of the block-long main street were the post office, the bank, and Dr. Webb's Drugstore. Along the street were several other general stores and a filling station. In the late summer afternoons, the men would gather in front of the filling station to play checkers, using

bottle tops as checkers.

"Every street around Leslie was shaded with huge oak trees. They were shady and beautiful, peaceful and calm. One street stands out in my memory most vividly and often I find it creeping into my paintings almost subconsciously. It was actually a shady little lane which went past Union High School. Often I went there with my cousins to play on the swings in the school yard. Along the way, it would wind, almost sadly, past the small cemetery where my sister, Joanne, was buried."

The hard-packed, shady dirt roads of Leslie seemed capable at that time of taking a growing boy and a dog named Tippy to the very best that life had to offer. Down the road past his grandmother's house was an area called "The Bottom," a flat sandy delta where spring rains drained from higher ground, and a stream slowed to a trickle in mid-summer's drought. There, in the shade of large oaks, and in the company of boyhood companions, memories were made.

"We would go down to The Bottom and dig what we called Toad Frog Houses. I later learned that the rest of the world called them sand castles, but to us they were Toad Frog Houses. We would spend hours down there building them. You'd put your foot down and pull the sand up on top of it, packing it down nice and tight. When you'd pull your foot out slowly, it would leave the front door to the Toad Frog House."

His constant companion in these ventures was his Cousin Lorraine. Being close to the same age, they would explore their world together and dream the dreams of childhood. A favorite place for playing was under Grandma's house, where they would often go searching for Doodlebugs. With a piece of broomstraw or a small stick, they would approach the tiny craters which abounded in the cool sand beneath the house. Inserting the straw in one of the holes, together they would chant the timeless rhyme:

Doodlebug, Doodlebug,
Home you must fly,
Your house is on fire,
And your children will die.

For the young boy who lived in Leslie, there were backroads to everywhere: to the spring hole out past the ice house, where on sultry days, it seemed that literally hundreds of kids played and swam; to the Flint River Inn which sported a real swimming pool; to Uncle Ishmael's house where Cousin Howard would skillfully carve airplanes from the soft wooden apple crates.

And if the road you wished for didn't exist, it was easy enough to imagine it into existence by simply crawling up into the big swing on Grandma's front porch.

"I had an older cousin—Naomi—who would always move into Grandma's house whenever I was staying there and she sort of took care of me. Naomi would get me in that swing and she would say we were going to Hershey Bar Town. If we could only swing high enough we would be in Hershey Bar Town. And we would swing and swing and swing.

"I guess I really believed it. I really believed that somewhere way up there at the top of the porch was a bunch of Hershey Bars…We spent hours doing that, but we never quite reached Hershey Bar Town. I suppose it was the strong anticipation that kept us swinging for hours."

There was keen anticipation, too, on those occasions when Jim's father—the cousins called him "Uncle Red"—would return from his extended travels. An excitement which knew no bounds would permeate the household. An almost ritualistic series of events would be set into motion.

"There were things that could always be expected. One thing we could always count on was a gathering of the family and a big wiener roast."

Uncle Red would go out to the chinaberry tree and dig a big hole while all of the children watched. It would be well constructed to contain the fire for the evening roast. Later, in the afternoon, he would set the roaring fire and let it burn several hours until all that was left was a bed of simmering coals.

"Meanwhile, we'd cut long sticks and sharpen them, all the while looking forward to roasting wieners and marshmallows. It seemed to me that there would be a hundred people there before it finally got dark, although, in reality, I'm sure it was just the family."

The best of times came usually after the wiener roast itself. Those were the times when the adults would sit and talk while glowing embers slowly faded to dark, one by one. For the younger crowd, it was the time for playing under the street light. The shouts would echo through the yard and down to the bottom of the hill.

One potato, two potato,
  three potato, four;
Five potato, six potato,
  seven potato, More.

Sides were chosen for a game of Red Rover or hide and seek and the hard packed dirt street would be alive with the sounds of excited screams and the pounding of running feet through the small circle of light cast by the gently swaying reflector of the street light.

5

"We'd play, it seems to me, till real late. Oh, Lord, I remember those days. In summer I went barefooted and wore only shorts—no shirt. After we finished playing so hard and it was time to go to bed, I'd go in, and my feet would be so dirty you could just rub the dirt off. I would be just filthy dirty all over, having run hard all day and wallowed in the dirt.

"And I'd be so tired and sleepy taking my bath in the tin tub in the kitchen after Daddy warmed the water in the open fireplace. He would give me my bath and get me ready for bed. And, of course, I would sleep so good…"

It all comes back as in a dream now, the cool sun-bleached sheets, the feather pillow, the tiredness of the day pushing one gently toward a moment between sleep and awake; the drowsy satisfied smile when night sounds play a comforting accompaniment to the good things of life remembered: the security of home, the joy of close friends, the white brilliance of moonlight through the open window. And the faint smell of wood smoke from the dying fire, fading …fading…yet hanging ever so lightly on the summer air like soft voices from another room. Far in the distance a train whistle blows against the mournful obligatto of a hound and the lone whippoorwill flies closer, calling farewell to the day that will never come again.

SCHOOL DAYS

It had become apparent by the time Jim reached school age that it was going to be much more difficult to continue the nomadic life which the family had followed up until that time. During first grade the family moved six times before Christmas, and Jim had been enrolled in five different schools.

"That was hard. Not only leaving friends behind, but just knowing that whenever we went into town, we would not be there for long. It also took quite a toll on my studies. I don't remember much about those first five schools; in fact, I don't even remember where I first went to school."

Finally, the decision was made that the family should settle in a permanent place. The place was chosen almost purely by chance, since it was the first permanent opening that the telephone company had to offer: Denmark, South Carolina.

For Jim and his mother it was a disappointing move. They longed to be closer to the home they loved in Leslie. Considerable discussion followed the move to Denmark, centering on the possibilities of a further move somewhere in Georgia, nearer to Grandma and the other kin.

"I think that Dad was reconciled to the fact that he'd come there to live. He was one who could make the best of any situation. He loved his work and did a good job, and he always made friends real quick. The new job as station lineman involved maintaining some 200 miles of telephone lines between Denmark and Savannah, Georgia. I think Daddy was thoroughly happy with the new situation."

Their first home in Denmark was Mrs. Minor's Boarding house, where the family of five shared two rooms connected by a bath on the second floor. It was a huge, white wooden structure on a corner lot next to the Baptist parsonage. Not a totally unfamiliar environment, the family had often stayed there in the past when travels had taken them through that part of South Carolina.

Although somewhat cramped, the new home provided fertile ground for putting down roots and a sense of belonging slowly took hold. Friendships formed and routines were established. In many ways the house and the town were much like those in Leslie.

"I can remember the kitchen with its light hanging down over the big table just like it did at my Grandma's house. The house itself was of the same nature as Grandma's except that it was two story. Also, in the kitchen was the ice box, a wooden ice box, and almost daily the ice man would come around bringing a nickel or a dime's worth of ice."

It was a true picture of the times as the ice truck approached with neighborhood children running along beside it trying to jump onto the running board. The ice man of Denmark was a husky, black man named Walter whose patience was unending.

"As he would slow down, we'd try to jump up on the running board and ride with him a little ways. I remember that as being something Walter would get on us about. He'd always be driving real slow and he was very cautious. After he stopped, he'd let us climb up on the truck and hold onto the side while he chipped off some ice for us. We'd pick up the little chips and eat them. That was something that every kid in Denmark, I'm sure, did hundreds of times."

Often there are memories that leave a taste that lasts a lifetime. This was the case with the weekly trips to the dairy for fresh milk. Carrying the glass gallon jug, Jim and his father would always go in the large room where the milk was cooled in a big vat.

"We'd get a gallon of that cool milk and on the way home we'd buy boxes of Oysterette crackers and that's what we would have for Sunday supper, Oysterette crackers and milk. My Daddy really liked that and I did, too. Even to this day I still like Oysterette crackers and milk. It was a Sunday tradition."

Those early school years seemed to leave only a few lasting impressions. The family's second year in Denmark saw another move, this time outside town to their first real house. It meant more room and a place for a garden.

The country was at war now and Uncle Red was forced to spend more nights away from home. At the same time, there were things that Jim began to discover about himself, things disturbing, yet seemingly uncontrollable. Change was hard for him to accept. Even the move a few miles from town preyed heavily on his mind.

"There were times there when I would stay home from school for a week at a time sick. Daddy would be working on the lines down near Savannah, and it was a hundred miles home. Since gas was rationed, they wouldn't let him drive back and forth. He stayed at a place called Scotia, a little town about half way between Denmark and Savannah. Those were sad times for me when he was gone, and I would manage to get sick and stay home that week for sure."

For the most part the boy's activities were closely tied to home, yet, images of these tender years in school come back now and again: images of a small knot of children standing in line waiting to go to the lunch room, or the image of what seemed to be the biggest Christmas party ever in the second grade.

"It was a time when I stayed very much attached to my family. I'd do anything to keep from going to school. My Daddy would let me out on one side of the school and by the time he'd get back around to the telephone office, I would be already around there telling them that I was sick and all kinds of things."

But as change became established routine, so was the acceptance, and what at first was feared, later was loved.

"I remember the second grade school room which was located right over the lunch room and in the back of the room we had a cloakroom. Miss Sharpe, our teacher, would make students go stand in the cloakroom. It was quite a frightening experience to be put in the cloakroom. But now it would be fun. As I look back, that would be the place to be."

In the third grade there were things called girls and one in particular called "Pee Wee."

"I remember how desperately in love I was with Pee Wee. I would sit there in class sending notes back and forth, and it would be something like 'Pee Wee, who do you love?' We would have the blanks after that for first choice, second choice and third choice. I was always third choice. I could never move up to first choice. I never moved down, but I always stayed third choice in Pee Wee's heart."

The years slip by in an awful rush, leaving behind the Pee Wees of yesterday. The feelings of youth seem to age far too quickly until one day we awaken to smell the honeysuckle of spring and look back at a lifetime of treehouses and afternoons spent playing kick the can. Like snapshots in a dusty album, we see ourselves catching a ride home with Daddy after work in the gathering dusk, or an all day trip on the train with a picnic lunch, or the remembrance of that day so long ago when you received your first .22 caliber rifle for your birthday and everyone taking turns shooting at a tin can. Perhaps the ache of sadness did more to shape our feelings and left the lasting impression that life can be tragic as well as lovely.

"During those years—I guess I was nine or ten years old—I observed some of my friends going through tragedies. I remember one boy—a friend of mine—

his mother died. I remember when they came and got him out of school and told him that. And I thought, my Lord, what a tragedy, what a heartache for him to suffer and I just didn't think I could ever bear those things.

"I was always fearful of something like that happening in my family. And then one of our classmates got killed grinding sugar cane. It was horrible. I was very sensitive to those things...and to anyone who would suffer. I always wanted to comfort them, put my arms around them, do whatever I could for them."

Thus, it is not unusual that he feels the most that can be asked of any artist is that he feel deeply the fabric of this life —its trials, its triumphs, its tragedies, its joy—and portray it in such a way that cannot fail to stir those almost forgotten feelings in others.

There are times in life that will stand out in the day-by-days of our existence, and we will forever after recognize them as turning points which push and entice us toward the full impact of life. Even as we live through them we realize without being told that these are things that matter...these are some of the best that life has to offer.

"Well, the big thing was to go from the sixth grade to the seventh grade,

cause then you moved to the next building which was the high school building. That was high school then...where the big boys were.

"We went from being big boys in the sixth grade looking down on the first grade, to being the little boys in the seventh grade with the juniors and seniors looking down on us. And they did torture our souls. They did things like taking our breeches off in school, always picking on us...scaring us. Seventh grade was probably not the most enjoyable year."

But for the youngster growing up in the summer of 1949 in Denmark, South Carolina, it turned out to be a memorable year. It was the year he discovered the love of an athletic challenge and an almost instinctive affinity for organized sports.

This was the year that Mr. Bob Zeigler organized the first kid's baseball team in Denmark with Jim playing first base. Mr. Zeigler had played at Clemson College, and all of the boys thought he was the greatest baseball player who had ever lived.

"We looked up to Mr. Zeigler. We respected him. He took an interest not only in baseball, but in each of us. Alone, he got the merchants to contribute enough money to buy some uniforms and put together a team. And he scheduled games all around. It was not part of any organized league, but we had uniforms and we had us a coach."

It was the beginning of what came very close to being his life's work. Throughout high school, he participated in every sport. He began playing basketball in the eighth grade. Tall and lanky, he developed into one of the best high school players the state has ever seen, averaging 30 points per game in his senior year and breaking the state high school record for the most points scored in one game, 71 points. He was named to the all-state teams in both basketball and football for two years in a row.

"I loved athletics. I did. I hate to think of myself as not having participated in it. It was the one thing I lived for."

In later years he would face one of the toughest decisions of his life when he decided to leave the world of athletics to pursue the artist's life. But that would come years later. For the time being, at least, he would ride high on the glory that only comes to the athlete when he is young and victory is sweetest.

The big part of athletics was all the fanfare that followed the game. The dances, the parties, the hayrides...all those things, as country as they were.

"My high school days were really important to me. I cherished them. I hated to see high school coming to an end. I don't know why. It was a milestone, I guess, for a time when you grew up and started getting away from home. I loved home. I loved the security of home, my mama, my daddy, my brothers. And I loved the security of high school because it meant that I still had Mama and Daddy, my brothers and home.

"I didn't want to see any of that change. I was a person who looked forward to the future only with anticipation of change. And I'm afraid I didn't enjoy a lot of things to the fullest, because I worried about them being so good right then, and they were going to change later."

One thing that would change later was Dr. Talbert's Drug Store. But before it would change, it would leave behind a world of memories for an entire town.

The drug store in Denmark, like those in most other small towns, was a center of activity. They called Dr. Talbert "Blinky" since he had a habit of squinching his eyes. But no man was any better to the young people who frequented the drug store, and the nickname "Blinky" was never used out of disrespect.

They spent hours in Dr. Talbert's Drug Store sitting in the old timey booths carving their names in the table tops. Dr. Talbert never minded that they did it either. Those tables were covered with everything imaginable. Everybody who ever loved anybody in Denmark would put their names on Dr. Talbert's tables.

"Well, those people who hung out at the drug store were called the 'Drug Store Cowboys.' I guess I was a Drug Store Cowboy because I did love to go down to the drug store and hang around. If you were bored and didn't have anything to do, you'd go down there and sooner or later somebody would come in and you'd go to ride with them if they were at the age to have cars. You'd always find something to do at the drug store."

The drug store would remain open at night whenever there was a basketball or football game, and if the home team won, Dr. Talbert would treat the team and just about anybody else who happened to come by. To look through the lighted windows at the booths was a scene that captured the spirit of those days — late forties, early fifties — days when there seemed to be a oneness in the community, a unity of purpose now rarely found.

To be young . . . to be a high school athlete . . . to be in love . . . it meant far more than merely what showed on the surface. It meant working together with classmates on the yearbook . . . or raising money for the senior trip to Washington . . . pancake suppers . . . Friday night football games in the crisp fall air . . . It meant swimming for the last time before your senior year under Holman's Bridge in the black water of the South Edisto . . . and it meant Saturday afternoon matinees at the DulaMae Theater.

It meant taking a date and going to the Drive-In restaurant where friends were sure to meet . . . it meant being elected captain of the basketball and football teams . . . and being elected president of the class for all four years in school . . . it was the Boy Scouts . . . the Beta Club . . . the marching band . . . and the terrible swiftness of time passing which would never come again.

"I was always inhibited by the thoughts of being gone anywhere for a day or two. I just didn't want to go off. I wanted to be home at night. I guess this sort of handicapped me in a number of ways, but has always been my nature.

"I didn't want to go to Columbia for the Beta Club convention because we'd be gone for a couple of days. I didn't want to spend the night at the river with the boys. I wanted to be home by night. I got homesick.

"At the time I guess I was a little embarrassed for feeling so sensitive about it. But now I am not. It's a part of my make-up. I have never really gone anywhere that I didn't want to go except to the Army.

"I have always stayed close to Denmark, South Carolina. I know that I always will. Back then, in high school, it was not so much the idea of not spending the night away from Denmark, I guess, as spending the night away from home. But, yet, that strong feeling I had back then is still with me now. I'm not going anywhere for long. I guess I'm lucky that I can be that positive about where I'm going to live my life."

THE ARTIST AS A YOUNG MAN

"The idea of college classes scared me. We had been told how hard it was going to be. We had been told during high school days by our teachers that it was almost impossible to pass. At least I had that impression. So I was scared. I was scared of the teachers. I thought they were trying to flunk anybody they possibly could. Some of them were...some of them were."

The longing for home and clinging to the good things of the past were feelings that continued into college and, if anything, seemed to gather strength. Dreading the thought of leaving to go to college, the young man now did all within his power to see that the things of home which beckoned to him so strongly were maintained and preserved.

"I wanted a college education, but I didn't want to leave home to get it. That morning or night before I was to leave for the University of South Carolina some 50 miles to the north, I wrote a note to my mother and dad and I left it on the mantlepiece there telling them how much I appreciated the sacrifices that they were making for me to go to college. I told them that I was going to do my best to make them proud. I sin-cerely meant that. And I was always aware that I was lucky that my mother saw the benefits of college education and pressed me in that direction."

Having visited the campus several weeks earlier and obtained a master schedule of classes, the freshman from Denmark went to his first day at college with a plan. Making certain that he had no Saturday classes and with extra heavy loads on Monday, Wednesday and Friday, he was able to insure that he was away from home for only a minimum of time.

"It actually worked out that on Monday when I got out of class, if I could catch a ride home, I didn't have to be back until 10:00 the next morning. That meant I could get up and start hitch-hiking about 8:00 and more than likely I'd catch a ride. If I didn't catch a ride, there was a commuter bus that ran back then and I could catch it.

"I didn't just go stay up there all the time. Somebody told me, 'Boy, you gotta stay up there and study.' Well, I just didn't do it. I was able to go home and study at home."

By the time basketball season start-ed, Jim had talked with the freshman team coach who invited him to try out for the team. For the moment, at least, it brought back the thrill he had known in high school. Although he was not picked as a "starter" he did make the squad and was playing a lot and doing well at it.

The thrill vanished, however, when the coach informed the team that he was displeased. Rather than allow the team to go home during the Christmas vacation, the coach informed them that he had arranged for the entire team to stay in one of the dormitories and practice basketball.

"That didn't sit too well with me. I had looked forward to the Christmas break. So I just gave it up and came home."

By spring, the young man's art career had begun almost without his realizing it. In fact, the origins of it reached even back into his high school days when he worked in his spare time under the careful direction of an old time sign painter named J.J. Cornforth. The older man, who often signed his work, "J.J. Corn4th," and the young boy, who eagerly carried the paints and brushes, made a good team.

"The experiences I got with Mr. Cornforth were encouraging. He told me that anybody could learn to do this with practice and it gave me confidence.

I became precise in making letters. I became confident. I wouldn't hesitate to paint on the side of a school bus. That required good lettering—exact. I did all kinds of things like that."

His greatest enjoyment, however, came from the work he would do with Mr. Cornforth on the large outdoor bulletins, more often than not on the sides of small country stores in the remote rural areas around Denmark. In the fall of one year, as the weather became cooler, they repainted almost a dozen of the large signs for the Coca-Cola Company.

He liked the challenge of leaving early in the morning to work all day scraping and repainting the huge signs, some of which were fifteen feet tall and perhaps thirty feet long. These were the times which whetted his appetite for the sign painter's craft.

"At lunch, we'd stop and go into the store and get a big Pepsi Cola—even though we might be painting a Coca-Cola sign—and sweet rolls, some cheese, and some bologna. And that would be our lunch. And it was mighty good. Even to this day, I enjoy going out to a country store and getting that kind of stuff. I can make a meal off of it and a pretty good meal, at that."

Frequently, while working on one of the large outdoor bulletins, the old

15

man and the boy would encounter other sign painting crews traveling the country maintaining signs for national advertising concerns.

It was not unusual for one crew to be painting "See Rock City," on the roof of the same store, while Jim and Mr. Cornforth repainted the Coca-Cola sign on the side of it. Or perhaps, on the road nearby, a crew would be erecting "Burma Shave" signs.

The crews, of course, shared a common bond. And when lunch time would come, they would sit together under the same tree and share tales of an era which was fast coming to an end.

"The tales that these guys would tell, and the stories that Mr. Cornforth would tell about his days in the Midwest, traveling around painting signs, just fascinated me. It was nostalgia at its best. I just thought that it would have been a wonderful time to live and a wonderful way for a person to work.

"Often, the conversation would run to the technical aspects of sign painting. We might be painting a Coca-Cola sign with a red background and white letters. Someone might say, 'Well, do you know that in 1920 Coca-Cola would put a black border and a black shade on that Spencerian script that they use for their trademark?' And may-

be they would argue about it or question one another about it."

It was a time when the conversation would run the gamut of the old time sign painter's art and the only prompting needed for a fascinating tale was, "Do you remember when…"

"It might result in one of the men drawing a layout on the ground or on the paper bag. Every time they would do that, I would get that piece of paper and I'd keep it. Or if it was a drawing on the ground, I'd copy it. And I kept all those things showing the various ways signs were painted. I had a wealth of information which I gathered during those lunch times working for Mr. Cornforth."

He showed a natural talent for the sign painter's art. So much so, that before he was well into high school, he had gradually severed ties with his early mentor, Mr. Cornforth, and established himself as a sign painter in his own right. Working from a makeshift shop in his backyard, he managed to build a thriving, small business maintaining the signs for a number of motels and other businesses in the area.

"One, in particular, was the Monticello Motel. A nice old gentleman from up in Virginia owned that motel. I don't know whether he realized it or not, but he helped put me through high school and college."

It was sometimes frustrating work. With no real work place or shelter, he was at the mercy of the weather. Without a car or any other means of transportation, he was dependent on help from his dad. But the job always seemed to get done.

His first major sign painting job, done entirely on his own, was for Lucius Wright, owner of a local dairy bar called the Frosty Manor.

"Think you can do it?" Lucius asked one day as the two of them stood looking up at the side of the building. It was summer and the heat seemed to hang heavily over the street.

"I think so," the young man said.

"I want it to say 'Frosty Manor' in big letters on all three sides; then I'd like to have pictures of sundaes and ice cream cones all around," Lucius explained.

It was only a short while before a large scaffold appeared on the side of the Frosty Manor dairy bar, and little by little the building was transformed into a newly decorated establishment. Later, the boy would go back to look at it again and again and feel the sense of pride as others viewed his work with approval.

"I always had a dream of painting the signs outside of town that said, 'Welcome to Denmark,' and I just stayed after the city to let me do that. I wanted to do that so bad I could taste it. But I never got the chance.

"And I always wanted to paint a big picture and put it in the bank. You know back then there were people who traveled around and painted murals on the walls. Now, I don't know; it would seem tacky what I had in mind doing back then. I used to go constantly in the bank and talk to the president, Mr. Jake Horne, who was extremely nice to me. But I guess he didn't want to hurt my feelings. He'd keep telling me, "Well, we need to come up with just the right idea.' We never did, and I never got to do that."

It was only natural that his interest in art would go beyond that of sign painting. As was the case with other endeavors in his life, Jim's mother saw the spark of artistic talent and provided the gentle encouragement that would widen his horizons.

On a trip to the state capital one day, Jim and his mother happened to pass an art store where he saw displayed in the window an oil paint set.

"I remember thinking that I had never seen anything so beautiful. It had two or three brushes and all the different colors were so neatly arranged in a wooden box. I suppose it must have cost at least twenty bucks."

It was a time of struggle simply to find money for necessities. But Aunt Buck, as his mother was affectionately called, went into the store and purchased his first art kit. In years to come it would prove an investment that would pay the highest dividends.

"It was really a supreme sacrifice for a foolish thing at the time. Twenty dollars at that time would have been a whole week's allowance for my mother to buy food, clothes and everything else. I didn't even know how to use oil paint. And I remember thinking, 'How in the world can we come up with twenty bucks for something like this?'"

If his work with Mr. Cornforth had been encouraging and bolstered his confidence, his formal study of art at the University of South Carolina seemed to be exactly the opposite. Only a select few artists, he was told, were able to make a living from their work. The implication was that he would not be capable of making the grade. The discouraging words came from art instructors who had never had confidence enough in their own work to try it and instead had ended up teaching.

The discouragement he faced, in fact, was so great that, almost in defeat, he changed his major course of study from Fine Arts to Education and set his sights on a career in teaching. In later years, it would come to serve as a strange commentary on the educational system —a system which almost destroyed an artist's career before it started.

It was a time when he thought little about the future and having been discouraged from entering the world of art, turned to his second love, athletics. As far as the future was concerned, he decided, coaching would suffice and teaching would augment it nicely.

As his senior year in college came to a close, so did the Korean War. It was 1958, and despite the fact that he was

exempted from the draft as a science teacher, the specter of military service loomed large in his mind. Having found a teaching job for the following year, settled on a salary and signed a contract, he decided at last that he could not shun his duty, and in September following his graduation he enlisted in the National Guard and left for Army Basic Training at Ft. Jackson, South Carolina.

Although the University had found little use for his talents, the Army was a different story entirely. When it became apparent to his superiors what his talents were, it was quickly decided that there was little need for training Jim Harrison. From that point on, he spent his days painting signs, posters and various other things. An entire week was spent painting the men's names on the heels of their boots.

With the onset of basketball season, the Army discovered another of his hidden talents which removed him from all other obligations. All he had to do was show up every day and practice with the basketball team.

On March 5th, 1959, after six months of training, he bid farewell to Ft. Jackson and returned to Denmark to finish his military service through weekly meetings with the National Guard.

"As I left the Army then, I was excited. Boy, I really had that behind me and I can truthfully say at that time I felt that those six months were the worst six months of my life. But as I look back on it, it probably wasn't that bad. I was in pretty good physical shape, and it should have been a time I enjoyed. I guess I did learn a lot of discipline...and a little bit more about basketball. But I was glad to get it behind me."

Returning to Denmark from the Army was much like returning for the summers while in college. With little effort, he soon was well established in the sign business once more while he began to look for a coaching position. It was not long in coming. He took an assistant coaching job at Bamberg High School only seven miles from Denmark.

"There was nothing really spectacular about my coaching career. I coached for eleven years. I coached football, girls' basketball and even baseball. I am right proud of the fact that as a head coach in any sport, I never experienced a losing season. I always had competitive teams and a winning record.

But, perhaps, above all else that coaching did, was to uncover yet another hidden talent. It was the art of motivation. On the wall of the gymnasium in one school, he had erected a sign which read: "We may not out score you, But we'll out hustle you." He seemed to have the native ability to instill a certain pride in his teams.

"I liked to work with children, to see them develop into good players. I felt that was my job, to get them to do that.

"The difficult thing for me was to tell a student he didn't make the squad. I was very sympathetic for the ones who were unable to make the team."

Aggressive approaches to anything had long appealed to the young coach and now, obsessed with winning and pushing his teams to their limits, he often found himself standing toe to toe with basketball referees attempting to gain a reversal of what he considered a bad judgment on their part.

"I feel like I was a pretty good coach and a lousy teacher in the classroom. One year I taught English and business math, both of which I was totally unprepared for and had no background in. I was miserable. I detested the classroom."

His coaching feats at this time were not going unnoticed by any means. Nor, at the same time, was he totally ignoring his talents in art. In fact, he was almost completely unaware that the two careers were now on an in-evitable collision course.

It began, probably, around 1964, when he was introduced to an elderly art teacher named Zita Mellon in the small town of Allendale, South Carolina. By the summer of 1965, he had become one of her full-time students.

"I spent that whole summer at Miss Mellon's studying. It was the first time I had had an art teacher who offered me some encouragement. I was learning things. She was an excellent teacher for me at the time, and I responded to her. I worked hard. For two months I was at Miss Mellon's studio every morning at 8:00 and didn't leave there until 6:00 or 7:00 in the evening.

"I painted and I painted and I painted. And she helped me. At the end of that summer when it was time for me to start back to school, I didn't want to. I wanted to work right on through the winter with Miss Mellon. It was the first time I'd had a taste of experiencing a little bit of the life of an artist."

Despite the fact that he did return to coaching, he always managed to find time for occasional visits with his teacher during the school year. And when school was out, he would once again take up the rigorous sunup to sundown schedule where it had left off the year before. The training continued for three consecutive years.

"It was at the end of the third year that Miss Mellon had begun thinking I could make a living from painting. I didn't know how and she didn't know how. Perhaps I could do it. So by the time I was going to another school, this time as head coach and athletic director, I was already thinking in a different direction. It was because of Miss Mellon's encouragement that I was thinking of art."

It was a tough decision to make. Not only had he risen to a new plateau in high school athletics that the college coaching ranks had also recognized his achievements. When the offer came from Furman University for an assistant coaching position, he was seriously considering it.

In the final analysis, however, art proved the stronger attraction. Even after touring the Furman campus and seeing the facilities, he could never quite see himself as part of the college coaching scene. At the same time, he was being urged by his art teacher, Miss Mellon, to try painting for a year. If it did not work out, they reasoned, he could always return to teaching and coaching. The decision, once made, was never reversed. Art became his life and livelihood from that day on.

HARD TIMES AND HIGH HOPES

"My Lord, don't come to New York for the sidewalk art show. There are plenty of them down there where you are. And besides, we have more artists in New York than we need," she said.

The voice on the Northern end of the line offered no encouragement. The voice on the Southern end, however, was the voice of persistence. It explained things slowly, but emphatically.

New York was simply the place to go if one wanted to make a living as an artist. He had given up a career in coaching and had allotted one year to make it as an artist. The only thing he knew to do was to head for New York for the Greenwich Village Sidewalk Art Show. With an air of finality, he urged the show's director to remember his name and "how slow I'm talking" so that when he arrived she might help find a place in the show for his work.

By the summer of 1970, he had returned to Denmark with his bride, Margaret, a former student. Together, they began housekeeping in a renovated old house, living in half and setting up a studio in the other half of the house.

"At that time, I had never talked to an artist who made his living from the sale of his work. The only artists I had been in contact with were the instructors at the University of South Carolina. They had never experienced what I was about to experience. They made their living from teaching and maybe sold a few paintings. I really didn't know what I was getting into."

With a small travel trailer attached to their second-hand Chevy coupe, the couple made their way to the City, camping along the way in rest areas and ending up eventually at a trailer park in New Jersey.

Meanwhile, his persistence did pay off. The lady directing the show remembered him and agreed to find a spot for him in the show. It was not a very good spot. In fact, it was the last spot in the show, on Bleeker Street in front of a village nightspot known as the Bitter End. The name could not have been more appropriate, he was to discover.

"Now, the Bitter End is a pretty good night spot for beginning singers and entertainers to start out. For an artist trying to sell paintings on the sidewalk the next morning, I'll tell you, there could not have been a dirtier place in the world."

On the evening preceding the show,

Jim and Margaret left their tiny trailer and went into the City. The fall air was crisp and cool, and the sights and sounds of the city filled them with an excitement which neither had known before. Walking arm in arm along 57th Street, they looked in the windows of the famous art galleries and dreamed of an elusive fame. Someday, they vowed, someday...

"That morning when I sat in front of the Bitter End, it not only seemed like a long, long way to 57th Street, it seemed like an awful long way from where I sat on that side street to around the corner—for a spot along one of the main streets."

Margaret could sense his discouragement. The thought of home was strong in both their minds. It was a moment when each of them considered giving up and going back to Denmark. He could paint signs for the rest of the year, then look for another teaching position.

Suddenly, Margaret got up and went to the car parked just in front of their space. A few seconds later, she returned to their spot on the sidewalk and got down on her knees. With a small whiskbroom, she began to sweep off the sidewalk in front of their spot.

She picked up the wine bottles, the cigarette butts and the waste paper. It could have easily been the filthiest place in the world at that moment. Jim watched silently as Margaret went to work on the sidewalk. A few minutes of watching her work was all that it took, however, to make him realize that action was needed.

"I realized that nothing was going to happen if I sat there. If she could do that, then I could do something. So I thought, I'd better shake myself loose and take a positive approach and do something."

It was the beginning of his first lesson in the sidewalk school of art. Leaving Margaret with the paintings, he began to explore the adjoining streets, talking with other artists. Despite its haphazard appearance to the casual passerby, the sidewalk show was highly organized, with each block under the direction of a block manager. Corner positions were highly sought after, since they took advantage of traffic on both streets.

Many of the artists he met had been participating in the show, occupying the same spots, for many years. One of those he met was a block manager for Houston Street, a rather well traveled thoroughfare.

"How in the world do you get around here?" Jim asked.

"Well, you have to work your way around here."

"How?"

"These people have been coming

to the show for years and years," he answered.

"Well, I don't have but one year and one chance."

After talking for a few minutes longer, it became apparent that the block manager took an instant liking to the young artist from South Carolina.

"Look," he said, "I'm going to try to look out for you. If somebody drops out or doesn't show up one morning, I'll move you up."

And that was the way it happened. A few days later Jim and Margaret bid farewell to their sidewalk neighbors on Bleeker Street, who seemed content to wait for fame to seek them out. For Jim Harrison, however, there was no waiting.

During the three weeks of the show, he moved several times. As other artists dropped out and went home, he stayed. He stayed and learned as much as he could. He was a beginner when it came to marketing his work and he acknowledged it readily. Even basic things like how to hang up paintings in a sidewalk show, he needed to learn. All the regulars had built portable, freestanding racks on which to hang paintings.

It was the little things that he had to learn, but together they seemed almost insurmountable. From one vagabond artist he would learn that to survive, he would have to paint faster.

From another he learned how to tack small pieces of carpet to the frames of his paintings to avoid damaging them. He learned that for many artists, the sidewalk was home.

"I found out that the people traveled around, and that every weekend there was an art show somewhere. They were all over this country. Huge art shows. Such places as Winter Park, Florida; Cocoanut Grove; Allentown; New York; Virginia Beach; and Las Olas Boulevard in Ft. Lauderdale."

By Sunday morning of the second week, he had gathered some materials from trash heaps behind stores and fashioned a crude set of racks on which to display his work. He had also moved up to the most populated street where crowds of art lovers passed by and many of them stopped to talk. But still there were no sales. Once more, Jim was discouraged and this time he knew that the quality of his work just didn't measure up to other paintings he saw.

"We were beginning to know a few of the people around us and after lunch one day, Margaret decided to go for a walk with the wife of the artist next to us. Well, bless goodness, they hadn't been gone long when a nice gentleman from Brooklyn and his wife came by, looked at my stuff, and talked to me a little bit. They walked off, but in a few minutes they came back. And he said, 'I have got to have that painting right there.'

"It was $85.00. He asked me if I would take a check. I was so nervous and excited. You just can't...nobody can imagine what a thrill that was for me. I had sold a painting in New York City. When Margaret came back, I told her about it and she was just as excited as I was."

Almost immediately he went to a nearby phone booth and called his old art teacher, Miss Melon. Then he called his family in Denmark. Everyone seemed as happy and as excited as he was. At the time he thought, it could only be a matter of days before everything would be sold out and they would be on their way back home.

Unfortunately, it did not work out that way. In fact, that one painting became the only one sold during their entire stay in New York. With expenses of $800.00 for the trip, the other side of the ledger remained at $85.00, thanks to the couple from Brooklyn.

The New York experience had taught him a valuable, albeit expensive lesson. He had learned much about the business side of the artist's life. Looking back, he knew that he had been ill-prepared for the sidewalk art show. With quiet resolve and the ever present determination, he decided to be better prepared when the next opportunity arose.

It was not long in coming. Within two weeks, the small travel trailer was once more on the road, this time aimed for St. Simons Island, Georgia. This show was for a weekend and it was much closer to home. He had painted a number of new pictures and was prepared to display them.

After three days there, both Margaret and Jim were sunburned and not much richer. They had sold just over $100.00 worth of paintings. The trip had cost $85.00.

"I wasn't setting the woods on fire, but at least I made a gross profit on the trip. I was a little encouraged."

But something much more encouraging would happen before they left St. Simons Island. They noticed that a woman had come by on several occasions to look at Jim's work. They could tell that she liked at least some of the paintings. On the last day of the show, she stopped to talk and they learned that she was Mildred Wilcox, owner of the Left Bank Gallery. She invited them to see her gallery and perhaps leave some paintings there on consignment. It was the beginning of a lasting friendship.

He learned from the artists in New York that galleries often approached side-

walk artists, but most of them warned against dealing with the galleries. Some of them told horror stories of being cheated by the galleries or having their paintings lost.

"I think that a lot of them thought differently than I did. They wanted to do their painting, and when they let that painting go, they wanted their money right then. I saw that in dealing with a gallery, you had to trust the gallery.

"I was willing to take the chance. I knew almost right away that there was no risk whatsoever in dealing with the Left Bank Gallery. Mildred and Bob Wilcox were delightful people, most trustworthy, and most interested."

The old excitement returned. It was almost equal to the feeling he had when he sold his first and only painting in New York. That night they returned to Denmark and the following morning he arose early, eager to paint. He was convinced by now that he would have to paint faster and be more productive.

"This was the beginning of some frustrating times for me. I didn't know how to paint fast. I had learned an awful lot from my dear teacher, Miss Melon, but I had not learned how to paint fast. I was taking two or three days to paint an 8 x 10. I didn't mind working late hours —and I really did. I was up at seven in the morning and I painted until seven or eight at night. I was frustrated. I was afraid."

In the middle of the frustration, however, he gained encouragement from Mildred Wilcox, who called to report that four of the paintings at the Left Bank Gallery had been sold. The call proved to be a shot in the arm and he began to work harder than ever before.

It was during this time that help came from a very unexpected source. While at the Greenwich Village Show, he had met another artist who signed his paintings simply "Drago." A Croatian, he had come to the United States to escape political oppresion during World War II.

Some five years earlier, Jim had stopped in Virginia Beach on vacation and had spent maybe fifteen minutes walking on the beach looking at paintings in a sidewalk show there. Those paintings he liked, he would photograph for later study. One artist he particularly liked was Drago.

Now, as he sat frustrated in his studio, attempting to teach himself to work faster, it was Drago who came to help. He arrived in the evening after driving 750 miles from New York. He was on his way to another show in Florida, but he had three or four days to spare before the show opened.

"Drago was such a prolific painter, and as he looked at some of my stuff, I told him what my problem was. I was simply too slow. He said, 'I'll show you...I'll teach you.' And that very night Drago sat down and did a painting for me. He did it in about an hour—a 12 x 16 of a boat against the sky. It amazed me how fast the man could paint. It amazed me and also discouraged me, because I knew how far I had to go to be able to do that."

But it was really not as far as he had thought at first. Later he came to refer to it as "hacking out" a painting. He came to learn that there was really no heart in it. These artists were merely repeating a formula—doing the same things they had done before. During the following few days, Drago set up an easel in one room and Jim painted in another.

What began as a visit of a few days soon stretched into a month, then six weeks. Staying in a spare room at his mother's house, Drago even displayed an amazing culinary talent, preparing an array of Hungarian dishes.

"Drago didn't have any money and I learned later that was nearly always the case. He was one of these guys who would sell $1,000 worth of paintings today and spend $1,000 tonight. He gave no thought to tomorrow. He truly lived for today.

"He always dreamed...he always told me that one day he was going to have a big show in a big gallery. But I knew he never would because he never planned for tomorrow. He was out of materials. So in exchange for Drago sitting there helping me, he also sat there and used my materials in painting."

It turned out as not a bad deal for either man. Drago helped him a lot. He taught fast techniques for painting skies and how to fade out backgrounds. He taught how to paint with only one color using various shades of light and dark. It was quite effective and could be done fast.

By the time Drago departed, he had left behind valuable lessons which Jim would use repeatedly as he joined the traveling art shows and began working in earnest as a sidewalk artist. For the next two years he would schedule his entire life around these shows. It was a time for paying his dues to the world of art, and he put in a lot of time on the sidewalk.

"I became pretty fast and pretty good at painting a few things. I could paint a sand dune right fast. I could paint twenty of them in a day. But it was repetitious...the same thing over and over. I don't know that it was so bad, but it was not what I had started out to do. I wanted to go out and sketch and put a lot of feeling into my work."

He soon fell into a routine which

consumed almost all of his time. Leaving Denmark on a Thursday afternoon, he would drive all night to save motel expenses. Arriving at his destination early Friday, he would set up the paintings and sell all day Friday, Saturday and Sunday. Usually it would mean driving all night to get back home.

With a minimum of sleep, he would begin painting again Monday afternoon to replace the paintings sold in the previous show. By Thursday, the routine would repeat itself.

"Drive all night to get to Miami; back home; to Virginia Beach; to Gainesville; to Columbus; Atlanta; all over. I went to some sidewalk art shows. And I guess it was profitable in several ways. Number one, I learned to paint fast, and after a year or so, I had ten or twelve galleries carrying my work. The checks were coming in from them right regularly."

Regardless of where he might go, however, home was always beckoning, and he never spent more than a weekend away from home. Despite the fact that occasionally there might be a show in Miami one weekend and another in Ft. Lauderdale the following weekend, he would always return home between them. He could not live the vagabond life entirely.

"I learned to make a business out of it. I learned how to go to those things. I learned all the ins and outs of it and I'm glad I did. I still have my racks, but I'd never go back to the sidewalk shows. I'm past that stage. But as I look back on it, I enjoyed it.

"It was a fun and festive time. I learned a lot about art…about selling…about people. And we rubbed shoulders with some really weird characters at times."

After more than two years on the sidewalks, Jim longed for the chance to slow down, to take more time with his paintings and do the very best work that he was capable of doing. The problem which arose, however, was purely economic. To achieve artistic excellence required time—lots of it.

"It takes me two or three months to do my very best work—two or three months on each painting. It's unbelievable how slow I am when it comes to painting, but I think through so many of the processes."

The answer was obvious once he decided on it. He would publish a limited edition print. There were several advantages to the print. Although the painting itself would take much longer to produce, with a number of copies made of it, even the art lover of meager means would be able to purchase it. And, of course, if all copies were sold, the artist would be amply rewarded for the extra time and work spent painting it.

Working for more than two months, he produced a painting which he titled "Coastal Dunes." With money borrowed from a bank, he had 1,500 prints published.

"On paper, you can make a lot of money with prints. Fifteen hundred prints selling for $30 each comes out to $45,000. Well, that's a lot of money. But 1,500 is a lot of prints. When I went over to Columbus, Georgia, to pick up those prints and they started putting them in my station wagon, I thought they would never quit putting prints in. I came home and started signing them and it seemed like a lot. But when I got out and tried to sell them, that's when I realized how many 1,500 really was."

Ironically, although he spent more time on that painting than he had ever spent on a painting before, he discovered a flaw in it on a proof copy, just prior to the press run. In the process of highlighting the clouds in the painting, he had inadvertently covered the stem of a sea oat. It would have been an easy correction on the painting, but it was impossible to do since the print was ready for the press.

"I showed the proof to some of my friends. Nobody else saw the mistake. None of them spotted it. But once I pointed it out to somebody, that's all they saw. I asked myself, if I bought this print and got home and discovered this mistake on it, what would I do? Well, I'd want my money back. I wouldn't like it.

It wouldn't be top quality."

Sadly, he telephoned the printer and ordered him to destroy the printing plates. The following day, he drove to Columbus and in less than thirty seconds made the needed correction on the painting. It was a mistake which cost almost $3,000.

From that faltering beginning, Jim's prints became some of the most sought after in the country. After publishing three more prints on his own, he saw the need for wider distribution of his work. At that time he approached a national print publisher and distributor, Frame House Galleries. Their only reply was a form letter saying they weren't interested.

"So one Sunday I'm sitting there and I'm reading that letter and I say 'Why don't I just take the bull by the horns.' I thought I had a good idea, so I decided to call the president of Frame House, Mr. Wood Hannah.

After apologizing for disturbing him at home on a Sunday, Jim explained that he had an idea. Up until that time, Frame House had published wildlife subjects almost exclusively. They were very much interested in endangered species of birds and animals.

"There's something else that's endangered, I told him; it's these old barns with signs on them and I'm interested in them. I think other people are interested in them.

"He liked the idea. I think he liked me. He liked the fact that I took the initiative to get on the phone and call him direct. He said, 'Why don't you send something up here to me. Send it to my attention, and I'll guarandamn-tee you that I'll look at it.'

"I said, 'Mr. Hannah, I'll do better than that. It's Sunday afternoon. I'll go out there and put a couple of paintings in the back of my station wagon right now. And I'll drive all night. When you get to your office in the morning, I'll be there. I'll show you the paintings and we'll talk about it."

With only one stop in the early morning at a motel for a shower and change of shirt, Jim Harrison was sitting there when Mr. Hannah reached his office on Monday morning. Thus began a long and successful business relationship due mostly to the persistence and determination of the artist from Denmark, South Carolina.

The story of what followed could very well be an important chapter in American art history. All of the twenty-eight paintings which Jim has done for Frame House have been sell-out successes. Many of them were sold out even before they were printed.

Possibly the highest plateau which

Jim has reached to date was also the result of his persistance and determination. Years earlier, when he and Margaret had walked along 57th Street on the eve of his first sidewalk art show, Jim had noticed the Hammer Gallery. They had both dreamed that one day his work would be there. At the time, it seemed like such a distant goal.

"I decided that the Hammer Gallery was the best in New York for my style of work. That was the one I wanted to be in. So I made my plan to try to get into the Hammer Gallery. It was simple: I was going to go there unannounced and try to get them to look at my work."

With a portfolio containing four or five prints as well as several original paintings, he decided that before going to Hammer, he would approach a few other galleries just to see what the procedure was. As he left that morning, he noticed that Margaret was extremely anxious. She was hoping so much that he would be successful because she knew how much it meant to him.

"I had the names of two places handling art similar to mine. I tried one and I got in the front door. I even got to the desk, but the guy wouldn't even look. He said they weren't taking anything to look at...they didn't even want to look at any. That wasn't too promising."

At the second gallery, the pro-prietor was at least more polite. She invited him in, although assuring him that she was not taking any work at that time. She did want to see his portfolio, however, and perhaps put his name on file for future use.

"At least she was encouraging. She looked at it. I hoped she liked it. I was almost afraid she was going to offer me a chance to leave some there. She said to come back later."

Later, however, he was knocking at the door of the Hammer Gallery. They were not too receptive. Did he have an appointment? Would he like to leave the work?

He was told that only Dick Lynch could make a decision on new artists and he was not in. The decision Jim made, however, was to wait. He waited for half a day, all the while insisting that Mr. Lynch look at his work. He had driven there from South Carolina and he would not leave, he told them, until Mr. Lynch had looked at his paintings.

Mr. Lynch did look at his portfolio finally. Right away he liked what he saw. Yes, he said, it was exactly the kind of work they wanted in the Hammer Gallery. As Jim hurried back to the hotel to share the news with Margaret, he thought back on the years of hard work and the long road he had traveled.

"It was an exciting time for me. It

31

was certainly a milestone. It was something I had planned as a goal, but way, way off in the future. I was very proud and very excited. I was in the Hammer Gallery!"

Within three years from that day, Jim would return to the Hammer Gallery for his first one-man show, "Rural Americana." During the intervening years, he had worked hard to produce thirty of the best paintings he could possibly paint. With an entourage of friends and family, he flew to New York for the opening and a reception at the Drake Hotel. By the time the show opened, every painting had been sold. It was the crowning touch to an exciting and meteoric career. Whatever future accomplishments may be his, that event will remain a singular insurmountable moment of joy and satisfaction.

"I don't know what else I could do to surpass that. I set a goal and I reached it. I now have other goals, other things that I want to accomplish. I'm working in new media—bronze sculpture, etchings, silk screen. I'm working every day to expand my horizons and to become a better artist. I really like to be just creative, and I'm hoping that these things will lead to new goals and new horizons."

EPILOGUE: OUR WORLD REMEMBERED

Thus, my dear friends, we have come at last to a place and a time where the road turns gently and we yearn to stop, if only briefly; to rest for a moment where the ancient tree shades treasures of the heart.

It is sometimes sad to think as we look back at the dusty country miles we've trod, that some memories are not as sweet as once they were. The world rushes on in a neon fury and that which we love tends to lose sharp focus.

The old sign on the barn is fading, its paint a mere shadow from a bygone era. The old man nods slowly as he rocks on the cabin porch.

"I have no regrets," he says. "Life has been good to me. Life has been good…" But as he welcomes the warm sun on his face and dozes peacefully, the thought will linger…Will we never come back again? Will we never touch once more the things of this life that really matter; the things that have brought such joy, that have raised our hopes so far above that which once we could only dream?

It is hard now to accept that these things will cease to be: that we may never again look deeply into the black pool at the bottom of the mossy well and greet the shining sparkle of cool water in a battered wooden bucket; or listen from the path that winds near the old churchyard as strong voices sing the aged hymns lingering in the air, muffled and subdued from a distance; or stand at mother's knee while she churns the butter, then pats it into the mold that leaves the impression of a rose; to stand in the misty

half-light of dawn as the nimble doe roams cautiously into the orchard clearing; to feel the warmth of the open fire on nights when the snow settles silently against the northern gate; and to listen at the window to the mourning dove as rain patters gently on the tin roof; to drink the cool waters of clear streams in the valley and hunt the wild flowers of spring.

These, then, are the things that mattered; all of these and more we shall sorely miss some day. That which we call tomorrow, will soon be yesterday. And if it were in our power to leave a legacy to generations yet unborn, there could be none finer, than to say:

Go down by the river in the
   twilight,
And stand where your fathers have
   stood;
Listen to the winds of morning,
And remember that life is good.

Jim Harrison
HIS WORLD REMEMBERED

American Byways, 18″ by 24″ tempera

Country Seasoning, 14½″ by 17½″ tempera

Tonic, 6½″ by 20¾″ tempera

42

666, 17½″ by 23½″ tempera

46

Unpainted Covered Bridge, 16¼″ by 24″ tempera

48

Clabber Girl, 20″ by 27″ tempera

Lucky Strike, 8″ by 28″ tempera

50

Brush and Bucket, 15″ by 22″ tempera

54

Burma Shave, 13″ by 22″ tempera

Snow on Window, 14″ by 18″ gauche

Liniment, 6½″ by 20¾″ tempera

58

SLOAN'S
LINIMENT

JimHarrison

Goody's, 14″ by 14½″ tempera

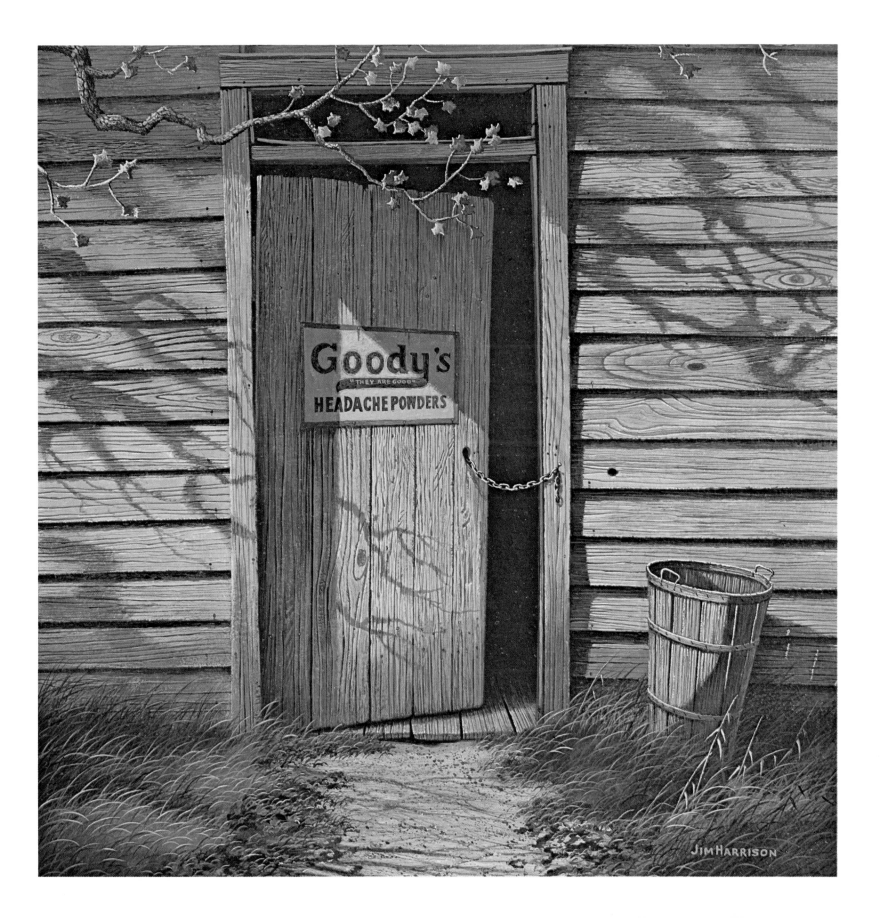

Bull of the Woods, 18″ by 21½″ acrylic

House and Barn in Snow, 11½″ by 15½″ gauche

Barns and Trees, 11″ by 26″ tempera

Coca-Cola Barn, 16″ by 20″ tempera

70

72

Bucket on Shelf, 13″ by 29″ tempera

74

Rural Delivery, 18″ by 24″ tempera

Woodpile, 13″ by 13¾″ tempera

Planters, 11″ by 14″ tempera

Jim Harrison

82

Guess' Pigeon House, 8½″ by 19½″ tempera

Martin's Station, 14″ by 20″ tempera

Dr. Pepper, 12″ by 14½″ tempera

Rural Americana, 11½″ by 20½″ tempera

90   *House on a Hill,* 9″ by 29″ tempera

Basket, 7½″ by 9″ tempera

Philip Morris, 13″ by 22″ tempera

Christmas Thermometer, 9″ by 11¾″ gauche

Red Covered Bridge, 12½″ by 26¼″ tempera

Guess' Barn, 9¼″ by 14¼″ tempera

Tube Rose, 14½″ by 20″ tempera

JIM HARRISON

Pigeon House, 10″ by 11″ tempera

See Rock City, 15″ by 30″ acrylic

House in Snow, 11″ by 15″ gauche

Nickel Coca-Cola, 14½″ by 17½″ tempera

Bucket in Window, 9½″ by 10″ gauche

Caboose, 17″ by 21″ gauche

Gold Dust, 12″ by 20″ tempera

Jefferson Island Salt, 8″ by 20″ acrylic

Tools, 14″ by 21″ tempera

Disappearing America, 15″ by 30″ tempera

124

House in Country, 18″ by 24″ tempera

126

Fallow & Forgotten, 13″ by 21″ tempera

JimHarrison

128

Pepsi, 11″ by 14″ tempera

7-Up and Blackeyed Susans, 20" by 20" acrylic